Marshall Kittredge Abbott

Myopia Songs & Waltzes

With Winchester and Hamilton Chat

Marshall Kittredge Abbott

Myopia Songs & Waltzes
With Winchester and Hamilton Chat

ISBN/EAN: 9783337180881

Printed in Europe, USA, Canada, Australia, Japan

Cover: Foto ©Thomas Meinert / pixelio.de

More available books at **www.hansebooks.com**

MYOPIA
SONGS & WALTZES

With WINCHESTER and
HAMILTON
Chat

By MARSHALL KITTREDGE ABBOTT

CAMBRIDGE: *Printed at The Riverside Press for Private Distribution*

M DCCC XCVIII

TO a mother of Sport, the MYOPIA HUNT CLUB, and in memory of the pleasant days spent with the sportsmen she has reared, this book is dedicated

PREFACE

¶

*H*AVING *been requested by several members of the* Myopia Hunt Club *to publish in some permanent book form what have been known for some years as the* Myopia Songs, *after much modeling by the author they have assumed this shape. May it meet the expectations of the "Chorus."*

The requesting parties do not seem to think they are worn down to the bone, even after their long use; and though intended to be noisy they certify they are not " roarers," are warranted " sound" without blemish.

If the author is not required to endorse the certificate, and the members of the Myopia Hunt Club *will accept theirs, these songs become club property, and the deed is recorded in this book.*

Perhaps, like old clothing, these Songs *when brought out into the air may be found " moth-eaten." However, with all the care of an "old clo'," they have been revamped in order to make them as attractive to the eye — and, I might add, to the ear — as possible.*

While applying the sponge and ammonia many pleasant memories of early Myopia *days were brought to view; and many a mental picture stood out in bold relief.*

CONTENTS

¶

	PAGE
PREFACE	vii
WINCHESTER	3
SOME WINCHESTER DATES	5
THE APOCRYPHA	7
SOME MYOPIA DATES	15
OFFICERS OF HAMILTON	16
HAMILTON	19
RED ROOM AND OTHER CHAT	23
APOLOGY	41
NOTE	42
CONCLUSION	43
THE GIRLS WHO RIDE	44

SONGS AND WALTZES

THE HORSE THAT CARRIES YOU THROUGH	49
WALTZ ROUND IN PINK	59
THE CUNNING FOX	69
THE WHIPPER-IN	77
OUR DIANA FAIR	83
FULL CRY	87
TO-DAY WE'LL HAVE A RUN	95
THE MOHICAN	101
AYE, AYE, SIR	111

Contents

SAILING OFF THE WIND	117
THE GIG SONG	123
THE MASTER'S WALTZES	127
THE CHEBACCO WALTZ	135
THE HUNTSMAN'S WALTZ	141
KENNEL WALTZES	145
THE REYNARD WALTZ	155
MYOPIA POLKA	165

LIST OF ILLUSTRATIONS

¶

	PAGE
M. K. ABBOTT . . . . . *Frontispiece*	
A PAINTING BY A HARD RIDING SQUIRE . *Cover*	
MR. H. A. ALLAN, MASTER . . . *Facing*	8
A BIRD'S-EYE VIEW OF CLUB HOUSE AND STABLES . .	16
MR. FRANK SEABURY, MASTER	18
MR. R. M. APPLETON, MASTER	22
FIRST POLO PONY BROUGHT TO HAMILTON	24
MYOPIA POLO TEAM 1895	26
MR. PARKER WHO SOMETIMES HUNTS THE HOUNDS .	28
VIEW FROM POND TEE.	30
POLO PRIZE CUP	32
THE COACH "CONSTITUTION"	34
THE HORSE SHOW. MR. DEVENS AT THE MEGAPHONE	36
THE LATE MR. L. M. SARGENT	38
MR. HENRY, GOLF CHAMPION 1895 . .	40
MR. LEEDS, GOLF CHAMPION 1896 .	42
A MEET IN 1884	46
"FOLLY," NOW 20 YEARS OLD	48
A MYOPIA MINUET	58
THE CUNNING FOX TO WHOM WE OWE MANY A GOOD RUN	68
JOHN CROSBY, "WHIPPER IN"	76
A BLUE RIBBON "DIANA"	82
MR. G. P. EUSTIS, WELL KNOWN MYOPIAN . . .	86

List of Illustrations

BALDPATE, NOVEMBER, 1896	94
SOME DEFENDERS OF THE "PINK AND CANARY"	100
A COMING MASTER OF HOUNDS	110
CLUB PUTTING GREEN. SETTLING A WAGER	116
VIEW FROM FIRST TEE	122
VIEW FROM THE ALPS	126
WM. CROSBY, HUNTSMAN	140
HUNT SERVANTS	144
MR. SHAW AND THE AUTHOR	154

WINCHESTER AND *HAMILTON* CHAT

WINCHESTER

¶

The Myopia Club was incorporated 1879.

President, Marshall K. Abbott.
Treasurer, Gordon Prince.
Directors, Charles Albert Prince.
Frederick Dabney.
Robert S. Jones.
William D. Sanborn.
Alfred S. Dabney.

Hounds brought from Montreal in 1881
Hounds hunted at Ipswich part of the season of . . 1881

SOME *WINCHESTER* DATES

¶

Myopia Fox Hounds organized 1882.

    Master, Hugh A. Allan.
    Secretary, Frank Seabury.
    Stewards, Francis Peabody, Jr.
            Augustus Hemenway.
            Edward B. Haven.

Kennels built, Colt's Leap, Myopia Club Grounds . 1882
Hounds imported from the Warwickshire Pack (Lord Willoughby de Broke, Master) 1882
Hounds hunted at Hamilton part of the season of . . 1882

The APOCRYPHA

¶

THE MYOPIA CLUB of Winchester was organized and incorporated in 1879. A club-house was built, and grounds were laid out in a moderate way. There was a plank lawn tennis court, which was one of the pioneer courts in this country. The nucleus of the Club sport was the great national game, base ball. This was played under unusual conditions, — being supported during play by frequent "wee nips" of Myopia punch, our own brew. It proved a great "mascot," and is responsible for many a victory and also for the birth of the Club. At any rate, as seen through the spectacles of time, it moved us to the idea of forming a Club, and no doubt the punch had its influence in selecting the name Myopia. Eyeglasses were a badge of distinction, amounting to a decoration. Many Myopes wore them on the ball-field.

The annual after-dinner processions through the club-house may be recalled, — a bath-tub for a bass drum. Though there may have been most extraordinary variations in the musical time of the drum, and great unsteadiness in the ranks, yet as they were never inspected by any military critics, there can be no doubt that at least they would have amused the Napoleons, and would have been reported on as unique, if not up to the highest military standards.

A Myopia omelette was invented; and the fragrance of its rich aroma, when it filled the nostrils of the bust of "Homer" (labeled "An Early Myopian") put life into the very clay. A momentary expression of delight, mingled with an air of gratitude for small favors received, passed over the face. With true poetic grace, no visible sign of aggravation was manifested, though it might have been excused, considering the "Early Myopian's" long fast.

At Lexington, near Winchester, an Englishman who had letters from a high English legal authority was entertained at a dinner. It was known that he was taking notes of his American experiences. Every opportunity was given him to study American table manners. He was joked in bad grammar and perhaps with bad pranks, and was finally honored by a Myopia land-slide. He was amused, if not somewhat startled, and seemed credulous when told that

Mr. H. A. Allan, Master

it was the greatest American compliment to a guest. A land-slide is produced by lifting one end of the table and forcing all the dishes to fall in a heap at the other end. This was an unusually prolonged one, as the table was long. The landlord's bill was also long, as a successful land-slide necessitates the smashing of much crockery. Strictly speaking, no defense of such a folly can be made; still a book on The Toasts of all Nations might convince the skeptical that in more than one nation glasses are broken after drinking. Besides, with all the everlasting talk some pour into the ears of travelers through our country about our magnificent distances, high mountains, long and wide rivers, and "great institutions," we were rather forced to emphasize the social side in some way, in order that the greatness of our follies might make the affair distinctively American. Shortly after this an English lord visited Boston; and wishing to send home to his mother "something distinctively American," as he expressed it, a local wit suggested "a barrel of Cape Cod cranberries."

After two years of base ball, lawn tennis, and upsetting the dignity of the plastic "Homer" with omelettes, Myopians began to sigh for new sports. As the printing-press and steam-engine appeared just in the nick of time to benefit mankind, so Hunting appeared, to interest Myopians; and it probably saved the name of Myopia from oblivion.

The sport of hunting was suggested at Winchester by Mr. F. H. Prince, who had followed the hounds at Newport. In 1881, hounds were brought from Canada to Winchester by Master H. A. Allan. Here occurred, on an unusually fine December morning, the famous "kill" when snow was on the ground, described by those who were there as having more of the quality of true sport than any other hunting scene they had ever witnessed.

Genuine "brushes" of the Reynard variety exist at this day which were once worn by Winchester foxes.

As the Hunt first passed through Lexington Green the pink was an apparition to the old town, rich in Revolutionary history. Old flintlocks fell from over the fireplace where they had lain for a century in their efforts to get into action. What might have happened is mere conjecture. The humorous remark of the oldest inhabitant as the Hunt proceeded towards the interior, that "'redcoats' when last seen on Lexington Green were going the *other* way," probably prevented a riot.

Some Myopians are perhaps not aware that several private packs of hounds were owned in New England at least seventy-five years ago.

The first case of a Boston lawyer, now one of the oldest members of the profession in the city, was against a huntsman almost sixty years ago. He started out to collect his claim, accompanied by a young legal friend, in the first chaise used in the Hub, which was considered very "swell" in those days. After a long drive they arrived at their destination, and were received by the huntsman in pink, just in from a successful morning, and their host, little suspecting their errand, invited them to breakfast. So lavish was his hospitality that they returned without mentioning the claim.

At Winchester, during the winter of 1881, there was a great deal of talk about a Myopia spring race meeting. The conservatives were strong in their opinion that Boston would not patronize racing, and that it would be a flat failure. But the "plungers" prevailed, with the true Myopian spirit of going ahead and surmounting obstacles. The enthusiastic agreed to back what seemed rather a gigantic enterprise in those days, and a steeple-chase meeting was advertised at Beacon Park, Brighton, in the spring of 1882. A long streamer "with the strange device" MYOPIA waved defiance to Boston Puritan prejudice against racing.

A party of New York men who had come on to Boston to ride, while in a carriage driving to the Park, were asking each other what "Myopia" meant, when to their astonishment the driver, with the usual "Beg your pardon, sir," in rather a didactic manner informed them that "Myopia" was derived from the Greek and meant near-sightedness. "You get inside, and I will drive!" was the quick-witted cosmopolitan recognition of such profundity by one of the New Yorkers.

So, after a long Rip Van Winkle slumber, racing was revived, and the new era of racing began which is now so successfully carried on by the Country Club of Brookline. The first Myopia Club races at Beacon Park drew an attendance of about eight hundred people; but as the purses were very small the guarantors were called on for very little money, if any, to settle all bills. The races at the Country Club are now attended by four to five thousand people, — about all the grounds can accommodate comfortably.

There must have lurked in the Puritan Boston of 1882 some of the Cromwellian strain (Cromwell owned race-horses and ran them), as has been shown by the increased interest in this sport. In 1882 the Country Club was organized, which probably was suggested by the possibilities of the greater field for racing and other sports under a stronger club, nearer Boston, Winchester being too far for afternoon driving.

As the Country Club absorbed the Myopia Club, the latter dissolved in 1883. The Myopia Club lived a useful life and did good missionary work in suggesting the idea of country clubs near Boston, and fairly earned the title of a mother of sport for this vicinity. Through the Myopia Club, racing was revived and hunting was introduced. The club was always active in spreading the glad tidings of outdoor life.

The name was preserved to posterity through the Myopia Fox-Hounds, formed in 1882, composed of thirty members. The kennels were on the Myopia Club grounds in Winchester. The roll-call of the Winchester battalions who are now members of the Myopia Hunt Club would not muster a corporal's guard; and it is a matter of deep regret that so many have resigned who resurrected hunting with a pack of hounds and who were the first to introduce a subscription pack and hunt club into this neighborhood.

As these recollections of Winchester are largely drawn from memory, the records of the Myopia Club being either lost or destroyed, they have been written under the title of the Apocrypha.

The glory of Winchester days was the good fellowship and brightness of its social club life. Bacchus will vouch there was fun there. The faith in Bacchus seemed declining until a Bacchante * was sent to us, which has been domiciled in our most beautiful palace, rent free. Is this a Jesuitic move on the part of Bacchus to gain a foothold?

---

* Since the above was written, the Bacchante has been removed to the Metropolitan Museum, New York.

The inquiry might be pursued further by asking if the Public Library is to become a bacchanalian headquarters.

But Bacchus is too late for Myopians. They renounced the faith years ago, and have embraced a new one. Inspired by fresh air and hunting they kneel at the altar of Diana.

But in these days of broad views the exclusive worship of Diana is narrow and sectarian. The modern sportsman is not content with a sport lasting but a short season; he must be a devotee to several, lasting through the year; he must have a demi-god which includes every form of exercise, — in fact, something which in a larger sense represents his ideals and fills his imagination. Therefore Diana is now a saint; and a god older than Homer — but, comparatively speaking, new to America — has appeared, whose temples are no longer slighted, but are daily thronged with the devout. All good, advanced Myopians worship at this shrine, and when spelt in large letters the name of their deity is SPORT.

SOME *MYOPIA* DATES

¶

Hunted from Gibney Farm, first season	1882
First Hunt Ball, Odd Fellows' Hall, Boston	1885
First Village Dance, Wenham Town Hall	1885
First Polo Game, Gibney Farm	1888
Dinner given to Farmers	1887
Ball given to Farmers and their Families	1890
First Labor Day Sports	1890
Gibney Farm purchased	1891
Coach "Myopia" ran season of	1891
Ladies' Annex opened	1892
Coach "Constitution" ran season of	1892
Hamilton Centennial	1893
Golf formally introduced	1894
New stables erected	1896
The second Myopia Polo Team won the Brooklyn Riding and Driving tournament for teams with aggregate handicaps not exceeding 20 goals	1897

  C. G. Rice, No. 1. G. H. Norman, No. 3.
  H. H. Holmes, No. 2. F. B. Fay, Captain.

OFFICERS AT *HAMILTON*

¶

1883.

Master, J. E. Peabody.
Secretary, Frank Seabury.
Stewards, Francis Peabody, Jr.
Augustus Hemenway.
Edward B. Haven.

Shortly after election Mr. Peabody resigned, and Mr. Frank Seabury was chosen Master.

1884.

Master, Frank Seabury.
Secretary, T. Wattson Merrill.
Stewards, Francis Peabody, Jr.
Augustus Hemenway.
Edward B. Haven.

1885.

Master, Frank Seabury.
Secretary, Francis Peabody, Jr.
Stewards, J. S. Allan.
George H. Warren.
L. M. Sargent.

Ten couples of beagles arrived, the gift of Mr.

BIRD'S-EYE VIEW OF CLUB HOUSE AND STABLES

George H. Warren. First year of "drag" with beagles. Hounds were used for hunting only.

1886.

Master, Frank Seabury.
Secretary, Francis Peabody, Jr.
Stewards, J. S. Allan.
    George H. Warren.
    L. M. Sargent.

1887.

Master, Frank Seabury.
Secretary, Francis Peabody, Jr.
Stewards, George H. Warren.
    L. M. Sargent.
    T. W. Merrill.

Shortly after election Messrs. Peabody, Sargent, Warren, and Merrill resigned. Chosen to fill vacancies: —

Secretary, George S. Silsbee.
Stewards, J. S. Allan.
    T. W. Merrill.
    S. D. Bush.

1888.

Master, Frank Seabury.
Secretary, George S. Silsbee.
Stewards, J. S. Allan.
    L. M. Sargent.
    F. Warren, Jr.
Captain of Polo Team, Archibald Rogers.

1889.

Master, Frank Seabury.
Secretary, E. B. Haven.
Stewards, L. M. Sargent.
  H. A. Allan.
  F. Warren, Jr.
Captain of Polo Team, R. M. Appleton.

1890.

Master, Frank Seabury.
Secretary, E. B. Haven.
Treasurer, G. von L. Meyer.
Stewards, F. Warren, Jr.
  G. von L. Meyer.
  A. P. Gardner.
  Francis Peabody, Jr.
Captain of Polo Team, R. M. Appleton.

A. P. Gardner resigned; James Parker was elected to fill vacancy. James Parker resigned; M. K. Abbott was elected to fill vacancy.

Mr. Frank Seabury, Master

HAMILTON

¶

The Myopia Hunt Club was organized December 16, 1891. Present were: —

    Frank Seabury.   H. D. Chapin.
    George von L. Meyer. Frederick Warren, Jr.
    Francis Peabody, Jr.   S. D. Bush.
              M. K. Abbott.

The Myopia Hunt Club was incorporated January 5, 1892.

OFFICERS.

Master, Frank Seabury.
Secretary, Frederick Warren, Jr.
Treasurer, H. D. Chapin.
Stewards, Frederick Warren, Jr.
          George von L. Meyer.
          Francis Peabody, Jr.
          M. K. Abbott.

1891.

Master, Frank Seabury.
Secretary, F. Warren, Jr.
Treasurer, G. von L. Meyer.

Stewards, F. Warren, Jr.
          G. von L. Meyer.
          Francis Peabody, Jr.
          M. K. Abbott.
Captain of Polo Team, R. M. Appleton.

1892.

Master, Frank Seabury.
Secretary, F. Warren, Jr.
Treasurer, G. von L. Meyer.
Stewards, F. Warren, Jr.
          G. von L. Meyer.
          Francis Peabody, Jr.
          M. K. Abbott.
Captain of Polo Team, R. M. Appleton.

1893.

President, G. von L. Meyer.
Master, R. M. Appleton.
Treasurer, H. D. Chapin.
Secretary, F. Warren, Jr.
Stewards, F. Warren, Jr.
          H. D. Chapin.
          L. M. Sargent.
          W. H. Seabury.
Captain of Polo Team, R. M. Appleton.

1894.

President, G. von L. Meyer.
Master, R. M. Appleton.
Treasurer, H. D. Chapin.
Secretary, F. Warren, Jr.

Stewards, F. Warren, Jr.
W. H. Seabury.
S. D. Bush.
A. P. Gardner.
Captain of Polo Team, R. L. Agassiz.

1895.

President, G. von L. Meyer.
Master, R. M. Appleton.
Treasurer, A. P. Gardner.
Secretary, C. G. Rice.
Stewards, S. D. Bush.
H. D. Chapin.
S. A. Hopkins.
A. L. Devens.
Captain of Polo Team, R. L. Agassiz.

1896.

President, G. von L. Meyer.
Secretary, C. G. Rice.
Treasurer, A. P. Gardner.
Master, R. M. Appleton.
Captain of Polo Team, R. L. Agassiz.
Stewards, S. D. Bush.
S. A. Hopkins.
A. L. Devens.

S. A. Hopkins resigned; George L. Peabody was elected to fill the vacancy.

Mr. R. M. Appleton, Master

RED ROOM and *Other* CHAT

¶

INCHESTER not proving a happy hunting-ground, the Myopia Fox Hounds hunted from the Agawam House, Ipswich, in 1881, and in 1882 from the Gibney Farm, Hamilton. Mr. H. A. Allan was Master and hunted the hounds. The kennels were at Colt's Leap, Myopia Club Grounds, Winchester.

In 1883 a canary-colored club-book appeared, bearing the title "Myopia Hunt Club." There were thirty members, and with subscribers the list showed about sixty in all. Mr. Seabury was Master and hunted the hounds at Brookline and Hamilton. The kennels were at Clyde Park, Brookline Country Club Grounds, and at Gibney Farm, Hamilton. The hounds hunted the wild fox at both places. Paper chases were also run from the Country Club, Brookline.

From 1884 to 1891 the Club was known as the Myopia Hunt. In 1891 a new constitution was accepted, and in due course the Club was incorporated in 1892, with the name Myopia Hunt Club. Its seal was dated 1882; its colors were pink and canary.

In 1885 ten couples of beagles arrived from England, the gift of Mr. G. H. Warren; and they ran "drags" from the Country Club from the middle of October until the heavy frosts set in, being hunted by Mr. Warren, who represented the Master at Brookline. Both packs were kept until 1888, when drags were given up at Brookline.

In 1889 fox-hunting was practically abandoned at Hamilton, the beagles were disposed of, and the hounds were then used for running drags. Drags at Hamilton were at first laid for a distance of three to four miles, but have been increased to such a distance that now a drag of ten miles is not unusual.

It would be an endless task to string the beads of all the runs about Hamilton and the neighboring towns. Those interested are referred to the Hunt "Log-Book," which contains very full up-to-date records.

Many would be disappointed if the fox-hunting about Framingham were not mentioned, and also the charming hospitality at Millwood Farm, the residence of the late Mr. E. F. Bowditch.

NORTON Ltd. BED-SIDE AND C.S. PAVILION

Cheapness at Hamilton reigned supreme; but no one grumbled at the loss of accustomed luxuries, as there was plenty of fun. Sport of the workmanlike sort caused even the *blasé* to burst out into flames of enthusiasm.

To men in the habit of rising late, the early morning hunts were a new sensation. The first "pink-coat" coffee at five o'clock, A. M., was far from hilarious after only a short rest. In these days ladies are conspicuous by their *absence* from early morning meets; and it is hard to realize the feeling of those present at the first appearance of the Dianas in the black of that raw, dismal autumn morning. It seems as if when ladies "touch our country their shackles fall." It was to many the emancipation of the Boston girl from the slavery of conventionalism to the freedom of the "new woman." Jogging to cover, there was an effort to be social, though awkwardness on both sides was apparent. The bows were hardly up to the Papanti standard; the talk was of the glum, monosyllabic order. But as the sun arose from behind the hill all was changed, and we warmed to the occasion and recovered our true selves.

The first Club polo game, which was also the first game of polo in the vicinity of Boston, was played at Gibney Farm. The so-called Polo Ground, a rough pasture rolled for a week or two, was not worthy of the name. If the ground was *bad*, the game was WORSE. It might be described as a succession of scrimmages. Occasionally the ball was knocked out into the open, rushed for by the nearest rider, *missed!* then another scrimmage.

So great, however, was the interest created by polo that the "hunters" began to quake, as they overheard some of their masters of moderate means threaten to take up with "t' other dear charmer," not being able to coquette with both.

Polo is a great game. By the enthusiasts it is ranked next to war. The "image of War" would suit us better, but as Mr. Jorrocks has spoken of hunting under this figure, out of respect for that ardent sportsman we forbear. In war some escape unharmed; but in our first polo battles it is safe to include the total of both sides in the list of wounded. The ambulance was in frequent requisition during early games.

Polo is no longer played with Indian barbarity and Indian riding, but is conducted according to the rules of modern civilized warfare. With improved tactics, and faster and more conservative riding, the "gallery" is spared many disagreeable sights which were of no interest to any except alarmed friends and the village doctor, — perhaps the patient should be included, though often unable to take any interest in anything. Our teams have won great games, and it is not invidious to say that in more than one

R. L. AGASSIZ   F. B. FAY   R. G. SHAW, 2   A. P. GARDNER

MYOPIA POLO TEAM 1895
WON NATIONAL POLO ASSOCIATION CHAMPIONSHIP

year the "blue and white" have played a strong game.

The Myopia polo team has never failed to throw down the gauntlet at Newport, the nerve centre of summer polo, in every tournament since 1889. Thus we have seen polo lifted from the merriment of a burlesque to the serious drama of a championship.

Some of the polo-field talk under excitement or disgust would appear far from pretty in print; but we will draw the veil. It is pleasant to record the carriage of the captain of a visiting team. As he led his defeated quartette off our field, subjected to the misfortune of a "goose egg" for a game score, he jocundly remarked, "A most brilliant defeat!" Such men are blessed with a temper which suggests the line, " Can make to-morrow as cheerful as to-day." The "to-morrow" *was* cheerful, as Myopians know, for he brought his team up to a point of skill that won victory, obtained his sporting revenge, as well as a reward for his buoyancy of spirit under defeat.

At Gibney Farm House the Red Room was born with all its fascinations, even to the ladies. May it always be painted red. Here the object talkers most do congregate, and the noise and din is such that even a stock-broker might fear to enter; yet it is very much like the "Board," all sports being dealt in, besides horses and ponies. In early polo days one member fairly became a dealer in his anxiety to have the best, and sold a condemned lot of eight for a lump sum. The minds of some of the Red Room oracles are *palaces*; they *know* what they know; they are hard-riding squires, too.

Dr. Johnson was a "cross-country man," was handy with his fists, and regretted the decline of pugilism in his day. If the shade of the learned Doctor should drop in at the Red Room during the heat of discussion, doubtless he would be pleased to discover that his own style of sledge-hammer argument "when wishing to drive home a particular point" is still extant. Nevertheless, the Red Room object talker is "true blue," and merits being Boswellized. Some writers seem to think that Mr. Boswell has rather overdone the Doctor. It is hoped that no critic will ever receive any support who tries to take Dr. Johnson out of the hunting-field.

May Shakespeare's epitaph, "Curst be he who moves my bones," confront any House Committee who proposes any change in the Red Room!

At one time time the Red Room had a great rival in the "Raving Ward." It was an overflow sleeping-room, which looked like a hospital ward with its rows of beds. It was also an overflow bathroom. It had a "splash" and shower-bath, both well patronized after a "run." Though the convivial glass will inspire the romance of hunting, it was demon-

MR. PARKER, WHO SOMETIMES HUNTS THE HOUNDS

strated repeatedly that a cold shower causes the imagination to run wild, and from it the most Munchausen-like tales of hunting experiences have been produced. The genial Baron himself would have found his invention dull here after a "run," such was the extravagance of the gasconade. One can read the Baron's delightful fancies in quiet, but a "Raving Ward" rhapsody had to be listened to while some four or five other thrilling experiences were being told, all with great emphasis and power. The aggregate noise was like the roar of Niagara. From this stentorian shouting the room took its name.

In the "Raving Ward" the Club crutches were then kept, and though significant of the perils of the chase they were seldom used. They stood in gloomy silence, with perhaps the pent-up indignation of wallflowers, watching the bathers perform on the stilts of high spirits, — the effervescence of a successful "run."

It is by no means from the dim past that the OLD "Chebacco" House looms up. The air seemed heavy as you entered the low-studded dining-room, with its chocolate and gilt wall paper, red tablecloth, and doily to match. Glancing about as one unfolded the doily, the surroundings caused a depressed feeling, —a sense of "carrying weight." A glass of champagne, and the "carrying weight" feeling disappears, in time for the inevitable broiled chicken, — always good, perhaps for being cooked over a wood fire.

The old "Chebacco" days had a great deal of "GO!" *Such* late dinners; *such* late hours; *such larks!* Who ever expects to dance again such Virginia reels as when the village fiddler tuned the strings?

We are now out of the homespun, and wear good clothes. Riders no longer dispute over the "pink" and the "blue." To be correct one's colors must be well toned down to nature. The feeling towards the "pink" on the part of the well-toned, down-to-nature group suggests the story of the Englishman who, when his attention was called to the color of our autumn foliage, said, "But don't you think it a trifle gaudy?" Though the "pink" may go the way of all things, many will part with it with regret. It is still the prerogative of the farm-hand who takes a short burst in the rear on the farm utility horse to wear overalls, with galluses, no collar, and his large bandless straw hat.

Golf has been introduced as a Myopia sport. Its development has been principally due to the efforts of Mr. Bush and Mr. Parker, who, in the opinion of many, have laid out one of the best inland courses in the country.

Myopians have now a new side to their characters. They have taken to golf *seriously*. Surely nothing can be more serious with us — except perhaps the judges at the Horse Show — than the earnest

VIEW FROM POND TEE

golfer. Members come into the Red Room after a hunt exhilarated, enthusiastic. The golfer is usually downcast after a round. Evidently to him "Youth is a blunder; Manhood a struggle; Old Age a regret."

To check the risibilities required quite an effort as the first professional golf match was played, so downcast were the spectators. The funereal procession wound over the hills and through the valley with an awful HUSH! Only the presence of a bier and the tolling of the village bell could have increased the solemnity. The following was overheard from the Pond teeing-ground: —

"I just drove over the pond with a putter!"

"Why did you do it?"

"Oh, in the cause of science," was the reply.

This is the only sunbeam that was ever known to penetrate the gloom of Myopian golf.

We no longer have a coach; but a few years ago the coach "Myopia" ran from Manchester-by-the-Sea to the kennels on polo days. In another season the "Constitution" ran from Pride's Crossing to Manchester-by-the-Sea, thence to the kennels. Both were a credit to the Club, being well horsed and well managed in every way.

Tandem meets in the past were very pretty sights, the first being under the guidance of Mr. S. Endicott Peabody. A feature of the second one was the Irish jaunting car. The ladies wore green; the gentlemen had green hatbands with flowing ends. It was all picturesquely Irish, except the brogue, which was marred by a French accent.

The boundaries of our success can only be measured by what we have done. We have won a National Polo Association Championship, which awakened our Club pride.

We have maintained the manly sport of hunting for fourteen years. We were forced to run drags because a large part of our country is covered with swamps. To-day the conditions of the open country are much changed by the use of the modern curse,—*wire*. A tangled web is being woven which may call for a further solving of the problem of drags. Drags have been developed to such a point that rarely a really bad run is ever had, and they certainly afford more fun to the hard riding "follower" than the pottering of early days. Some students of the "drags" claim they will yet be able to give them all the features of wild fox-hunting. We hope their efforts may prove successful. A past member of our Club, for many years Master of a hunt near New York, has tried every known artificial scent with varying success. With Darwinian research he has evolved a science, and has proved a natural selection of scents adapted to the different atmospheric conditions.

The Judge, the village legal dignitary, once said

...morning tea. The ladies wore green, and all had green hatbands with flowing ends. It was all picturesquely Irish, except the brogue, which was marred by a French accent.

The boundaries of our success can only be measured by what we have done. We have won a National Association Championship, which awakened our Club pride.

We have maintained the manly sport of hunting for fourteen years. We were forced to use drags because a large part of our country is covered with swamps. To-day the conditions of the open country are much changed by the recent too modern curse,—*wire*. A tangled web is being woven which may call for a fiercer solving of the problem of drags. Drags have been developed to such a point that rarely a really bad run is ever had, and certainly afford more fun to the hard riding "follower" than the pottering of early days. Some students of the "drags" claim they will yet be able to give them all the features of wild fox hunting. We hope their efforts may prove successful. A past member of our Club, for many years Master of a hunt near New York, has tried every known artificial scent with varying success. With Darwinian research he has evolved a science, and has proved a natural selection of scents adapted to the different atmospheric conditions.

The Judge, the village legal dignitary or a paid

POLO PRIZE CUP

that hunting was one of the important industries of Hamilton. Though said in jest, his remark contains considerable truth, for the village has reaped some advantage, as will be shown.

Speaking of hunting as an industry, many will be surprised to learn that according to Badminton there are altogether over three hundred packs of staghounds, foxhounds, harriers, and beagles in England, Ireland, and Scotland. A few years ago a Boston daily paper appeared with an article showing an investment in England alone of about twenty millions of dollars for these sports. Perhaps in this country an estimate of one million dollars for hunting and polo is not an excessive amount. This includes the various Club properties connected with the sports. Golf threatens to become a rival of the bicycle industry in the amount of capital invested. Every village and town feels the necessity of a golf-course in the pursuit of happiness.

When country people become aware of these facts we may expect rival villages to compete for the settlement of Hunt Clubs in their midst. In the competition we are prepared to hear that the selectmen offer a house free of rent for the Master. As in the case of other industries, of course the Club property will be exempt from taxes for five years. Restrictions on barbed wire might be made by the selectmen. Negotiators for Hunt Club sites must not be deceived by popular sentiment against electric railroads. This is sure to change, and is always likely to spoil any New England village when least expected.

We have run the gamut of Labor Day sports, beginning with races on the flat and steeple-chases, also "point to point" races, to amuse the farmers and their families. The Princemere christening was a very interesting race meeting, at which the turnouts were unusually smart, and on the whole was a picture with a charm which the Shore has not since reproduced. Then followed in other years a series of Gymkhana Games. In 1896 the first Horse Show was held on the polo ground. Through this show the Club put themselves in touch with the farmers and villagers, who were highly entertained and turned out in force. There were about two hundred entries. The judges were busy all day long, and an interested crowd remained through the twilight until dark, determined to see the last jump taken. Ladies accustomed to riding straight to hounds competed for the prizes, and two of the fair captured blue ribbons. This was a matter of pride to all Myopians.

Music on Sunday afternoons for the entertainment of the ladies was kept up for many years, by the favor of Master Seabury. An ambitious attempt to introduce full band concerts on Sundays was frowned down by the conservative element. Spirited dances at the Annex for members have been given. Christ-

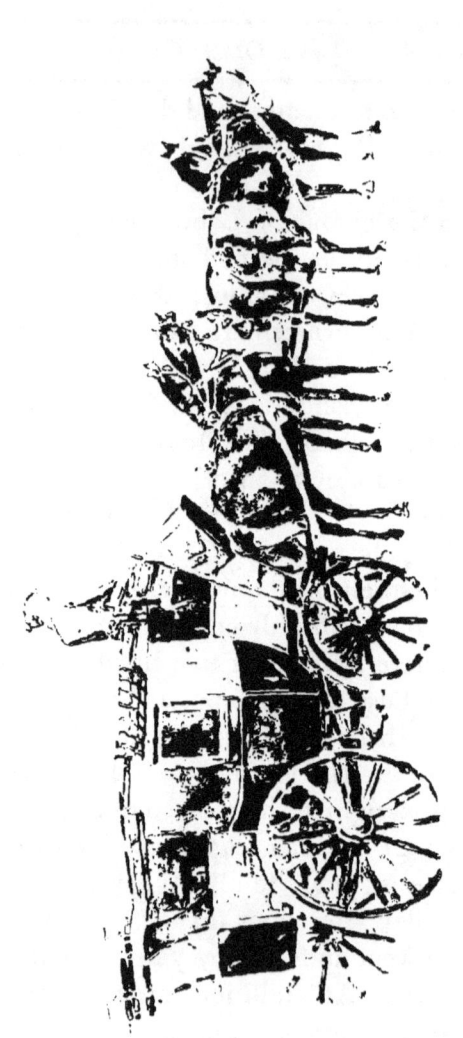

mas trees and Christmas dinners to village children are still in vogue, and long may they prevail.

All Myopians, besides enjoying sport, enjoy nature. To quote from what Carlyle called the "ghastly" science of political economy, nature never whispers anything about Taxes. Still it is admitted that Taxes are necessary to the social order. Myopians at Hamilton are very close to nature in this respect, as Taxes are very low; and this is due indirectly to the Myopia Hunt Club. The farmers are very generous in allowing us to ride over their lands, and many of them have sporting tendencies. Doubtless they are pleased at lower tax rates and the increasing values of real estate. It is to be hoped that these factors have their influence in soothing their irritation whenever an overlooked broken rail is not replaced by a sound one.

Though it is claimed that parsimony is a fundamental principle in nature, yet to the casual observer she is at times quite prodigal, and furnishes sufficient ground for those who are not close students of natural laws to indulge in a little conservative sporting extravagance. Sport is considered by many to be a waste of money, and probably not a few of the devotees of Carlyle's "ghastly" science think the sums spent ought to be added to Capital.

We differ from this view; because some few in a community are benefited — they are consumers and must buy! Besides, it pleases the Myopian to see the nimble sixpence "get a move on," to use a race-track phrase. Myopians are all altruistic, and though their contributions to the general good are filtered through selfishness, they regard their sporting outgo from an altruistic standpoint.

There is no living Myopian example of the highest altruistic flights who prefers to peddle out his fortune little by little at a *loss* in order to look his fellow man in the face and call him "Brother"! Born in thrifty New England, it is bred into the very bones of Myopians to transact affairs for GAIN. They recognize no benevolence in trade; and so robust is their conviction that many generations must pass before their consciences become so sick that they will spend all that they have, *even for Sport*, to attain altruistic bliss.

The Myopians of 1882, intent on their sport, had no idea that their presence would have any effect on the village of Hamilton, which has improved so much in general appearance as to call out the comment of people who knew it then; and as to feeling they would be factors in influencing in any way such stupendous problems as Real Estate and Taxes, — it was farthest from their thoughts. The Village Improvement Society goes on with the good work.

The Press has exhausted its joke and satire, sometimes amusing and sometimes rather bitter; and it

THE HORSE SHOW. MR. DEVENS
AT THE MEGAPHONE

now defends polo and other sports, and publishes in the society items the rather monotonous news about "breakfasts" with good grace.

But it is hardly within the scope of this rough sketch to enumerate all our achievements.

It is rather remarkable that after long wanderings so many Myopians should return to historic Essex County from which their ancestors went to seek their fortunes a century ago. In locating here they have undoubtedly increased their usefulness, and the community has been benefited. It is argued by students of the question that the settling of city people in our villages is of mutual advantage to both. Each can learn much of the other, as both at the start are apt to be misunderstood. Hamilton is an instance of the best results obtained by this blending.

English country life is a relic of the feudal system; but no such conditions exist in New England. Simplicity is most prominent at Hamilton. Though the leaps from city luxury to Hamiltonian simplicity are wide, all seem to land safely and to enjoy life even more on the "landing side." It may be asked if we are advancing in the path of the simplicity claimed for uncivilized tribes, who for "honesty, amiability, self-government, and freedom are examples to communities more advanced." We are unable to answer. But it is hoped that boys growing up here will prefer horses and ponies rather than the bow and arrow or the javelin, instruments of sport, which always seem to accompany the simplicity of the uncivilized.

The temperature of club life might be raised in winter. Why not give Jack Frost a more conspicuous niche in the temple of Sport? High carnival might reign in his court, and our cup would be filled.

It was once proposed to change our name "Myopia." If we had made the change, it would have been at the expense of a great deal of free advertising. Unhappy is the man who knows not the soothing influence of "Myopia cigars." With what pride we read the glaring announcement in the bar-room windows, "Choice Myopia Club Whiskey" — yet unknown to Myopians. Perhaps the superintendent has his suspicions as to the quality! Shop windows in New York are filled with Myopia neckties, and yet no Boston haberdasher has yet complimented us with any such wares. Such is fame — near home!

But it may be said, "Why so many reminiscences? We asked for songs!" Read your Badminton and notice the reverential antiquarian spirit with which the writer speaks of groping into the dark ages of the Quorn, whose glory dates from 1753. We do not date back, to be sure, but why not make the most of our existence? Besides, a history of the Myopia may be written in the future, and this vol-

THE LATE MR. J. M. SARGENT

ume may then be yellow-leaved, musty, and enveloped in the glamour of age, and with all its vagaries may prove the very Genesis of the Myopia Hunt Club. Besides, the old squires will enjoy fighting their battles over again. If one pleasant recollection here revived suggests another, they have not been written in vain.

We have had our shining lights, to whom the country listens when addressed. Others are known by their writings. Some have won an "Hon.," and more titles are in view. Some are pressing into the front ranks in their professions. The mainstay of the Club is the work-hard-and-play-hard business man. Some of the brightest stars are no longer visible in the Myopian firmament, — "tho' lost to sight, to memory dear."

We have groped along in a Myopic way; we have added polo and golf to our sport, and though there is no increase of riders in the hunting field, and no increase of polo players, yet golf has added very much to the life of the Club and also to the grounds. The improved appearance of the Club grounds is also due to golf. They are no longer clad in russet brown of the earlier days, but wear their new mantle of bright green. The landscape effect might be heightened by the addition of more picturesque shepherds of the Watteau variety. We are fortunate in having an interesting golf course, which undoubtedly will be fast when "tuned up."

Though the Myopia Hunt Club is only a sapling, the prospects of becoming a tree were never brighter than now, for the reason that the interest in sport is increasing, and the leisure contingent is growing. To use the latest definition—"Leisure consists in the diligent and intelligent use of time." When lived up to on these lines, leisure ought to be considered highly respectable, though the comment is sometimes harsh. Men of leisure cannot be drones. Those who had earned a competency used to take their ease; though a rich retired soap-maker once applied to his successors for permission to assist at the soap-boiling on boiling days. This seems to be doing a sort of penance for idleness. But now we have golf, with its never-ceasing interest and adapted to all ages, which is the panacea of all ills of body and soul; and the retired need not sigh for the "shop." New England is fast becoming the play-ground of this country for the leisure element. A sporting colony is their paradise, and we are likely to receive our share of their support.

Everything within the limits of the Club purse is being expended to improve the sporting facilities. With such an able management as we have, who give up much valuable time for the benefit of members, the Myopia Hunt Club is sure to preserve its attractions, and—though perhaps it may be hard for old members to admit it—may have a future even more interesting than its past.

MR. HENRY, GOLF CHAMPION 1895

APOLOGY

¶

IF the chorus is not hoarse (no pun intended), with profound apologies to the strictly hunting set of the Myopia Hunt Club, a few Yachting Songs are introduced. Doubtless many in the Club will be reminded of "jolly old yachting days," — the days of the Fortuna, Phantom, Mohican, Active, Maggie, Addie, North Star, — and the Bayadere, owned by "Squire" Merrill. The "Squire" was one of the first to mount his hunter in answer to the call of his country (Myopia) to repel the invasion of the enemy (Reynard).

NOTE

¶

THE author, as you have doubtless discovered, — or will discover, — is not truly musical. Nothing is claimed except an intimacy with the key of C, which never ripened into a friendship, as the key of C was unmercifully pummeled to extract the airs. In fact the piano keys fairly trembled when approached, showing that even music has its brute side. If the airs are not what they should be, it is not the fault of the key of C or the piano, but a case of a "bad man on a good horse."

In view of these facts, why not organize a "Society for the Prevention of Banging Pianos"? Why not have heavy fines for discords? There would be no lack of voluntary lobbying at the State House to bring about a pressure for the passage of such laws. *Because of this lack of musical knowledge, the writing of the music and arrangement of waltzes has been left to others.*

CONCLUSION

¶

BUT you are weary? There will be no attempt at a graceful literary "finish," no conciliation or defiance of critics, though it may not be amiss for the author to express his regret that this work has not been committed to more competent hands.

As "discretion is the truest valor" and always sportsmanlike, considering that the mount is "green," and the pastures heavy and "trappy," it may be prudent to "pull out." The author therefore decides not to "go through;" and he parts company from those who have "followed" in this "run" with its variety of country, leaving it to them to increase the glory of **THE MYOPIA HUNT CLUB**.

¶

Make "this subject for heroic song;"
The author's trifles may not last long.
Excel in sport, and "merry, merry be;"
Dance the "tipsy dance of jollity;"
Let chats of hunting, golf, polo, race,
Find the Dr. Johnsons in their place!

THE GIRLS WHO RIDE

␣N mettled hunter seated firm,
In form and grace complete,
The dullest heart will light and burn
As we the fair Dianas greet.
No picture is their peer,
For Art must stand aside;
For them I shout my cheer, —
Hurrah for the girls who ride!

In salon they may smile
Or look demure and sweet,
But glances cannot so beguile
As those that grace the "meet;"
Fresh air and riding are blended wine
On hunters of easy stride;
Drink, drink, the vintage rich, divine!
Hurrah for the girls who ride!

With cheek aglow and flashing eye,
Their faces with radiance lit, —

Brave knights for them would die,
Of danger's cup would sip;
For the world loves pluck
And courage in peril tried;
We love them and wish them luck; —
God bless the girls who ride!

Riding is a symphony
Most soothing to the mind,
Brings body and soul in harmony, —
No discord can you find;
So then in manly chorus
Let it swell like the ocean tide,
With voices strong, sonorous, —
Hosannas for the girls who ride!

A MEET IN 1884

SONGS & WALTZES

THE HORSE THAT CARRIES YOU THROUGH

THE HORSE THAT CARRIES YOU THROUGH

THE HORSE THAT CARRIES YOU THROUGH

THE HORSE THAT CARRIES YOU THROUGH

LINDA VISTA

WALTZ ROUND IN PINK

WALTZ ROUND IN PINK

61

WALTZ ROUND IN PINK

WALTZ ROUND IN PINK

THE CUNNING FOX TO WHOM WE OWE MANY A GOOD RUN

THE CUNNING FOX

THE CUNNING FOX

THE CUNNING FOX

THE CUNNING FOX

Of a frost-y morn I'm sly, I

noth-ing fool-ish try, 'Ware hounds at break of day; . . . But

74 THE CUNNING FOX

THE CUNNING FOX

JOHN CROSBY, "WHIPPER-IN"

THE WHIPPER-IN

THE WHIPPER-IN

THE WHIPPER-IN

THE WHIPPER-IN

A BLUE RIBBON - DIANA

OUR DIANA FAIR

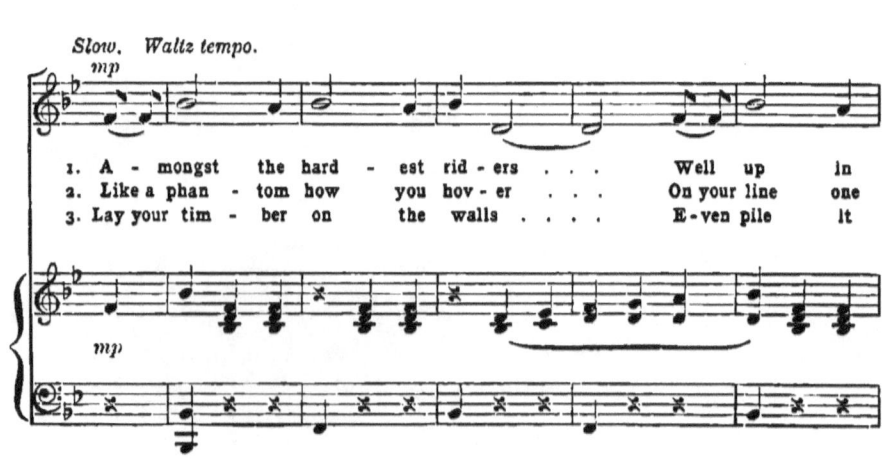

1. A - mongst the hard - est rid - ers ... Well up in
2. Like a phan - tom how you hov - er ... On your line one
3. Lay your tim - ber on the walls ... E - ven pile it

the first flight ... Nev - er with out - sid - ers ... But
side the hounds ... We all be - come fond lov - ers ... As
to the sky ... Our la - dy heeds not falls, ...

MR. G. P. EUSTIS, WELL-KNOWN MAYORAL

FULL CRY

REFRAIN.
mf a tempo.

Tal-ly Ho! Hark, a-way! To mel-o-dy and May.

Down in our sad-dles deep, The strong-est of seats. Tal-ly

Ho, Hark, a-way! To mel-o-dy and May.

Down in our sad-dles deep, The strong-est of seats.

FULL CRY

FULL CRY

BALDPATE, NOV. 1967

TO-DAY WE'LL HAVE A RUN

TO-DAY WE'LL HAVE A RUN

THE MOHICAN

more you pad - dle your ca - noe, Yet a Mo - hi - can sails the o - cean blue.

CHORUS.

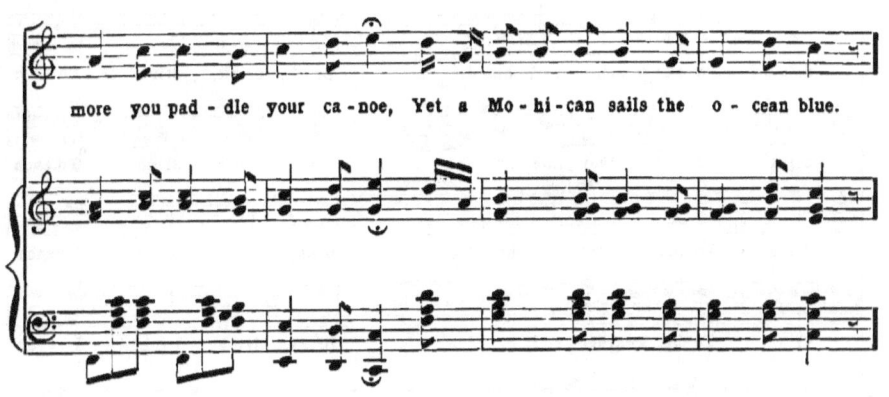

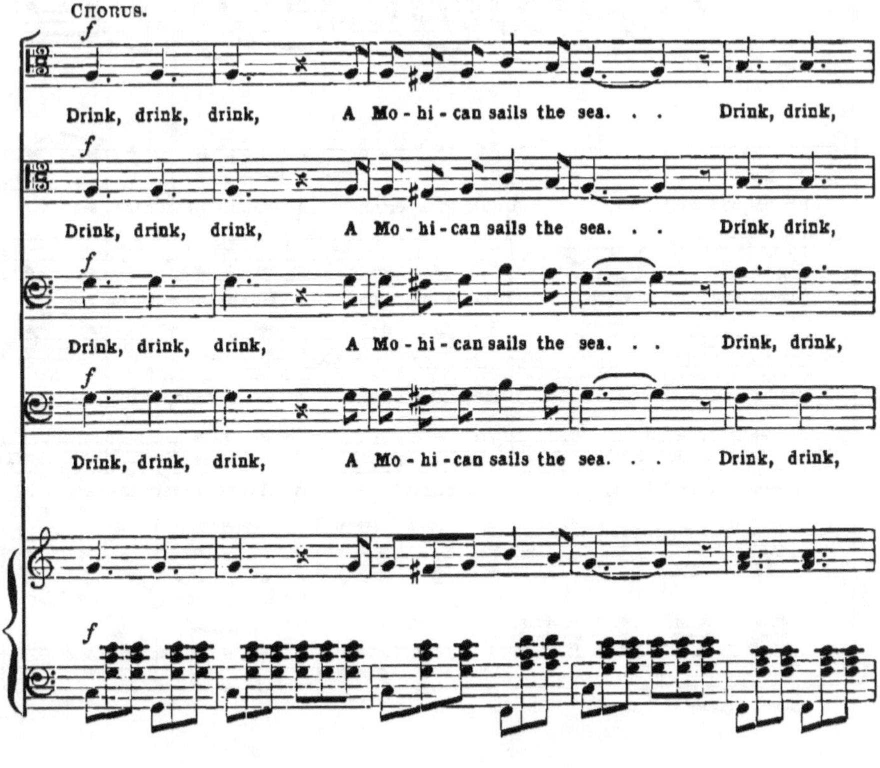
f
Drink, drink, drink, A Mo - hi - can sails the sea. . . Drink, drink,
f
Drink, drink, drink, A Mo - hi - can sails the sea. . . Drink, drink,
f
Drink, drink, drink, A Mo - hi - can sails the sea. . . Drink, drink,
f
Drink, drink, drink, A Mo - hi - can sails the sea. . . Drink, drink,
f

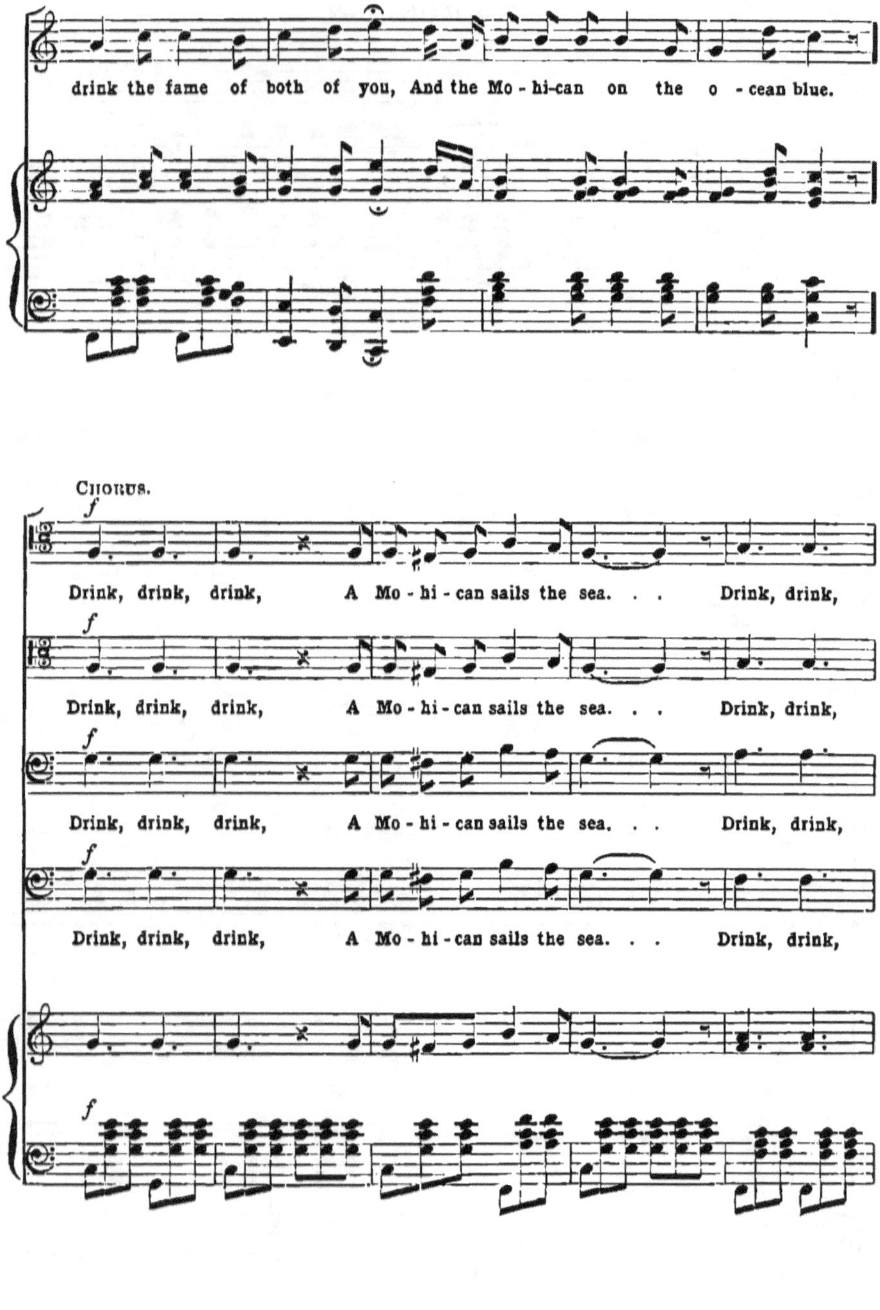
drink the fame of both of you, And the Mo - hi-can on the o - cean blue.
Chorus.
f
Drink, drink, drink, A Mo - hi - can sails the sea. . . Drink, drink,
f
Drink, drink, drink, A Mo - hi - can sails the sea. . . Drink, drink,
f
Drink, drink, drink, A Mo - hi - can sails the sea. . . Drink, drink,
f
Drink, drink, drink, A Mo - hi - can sails the sea. . . Drink, drink,
f

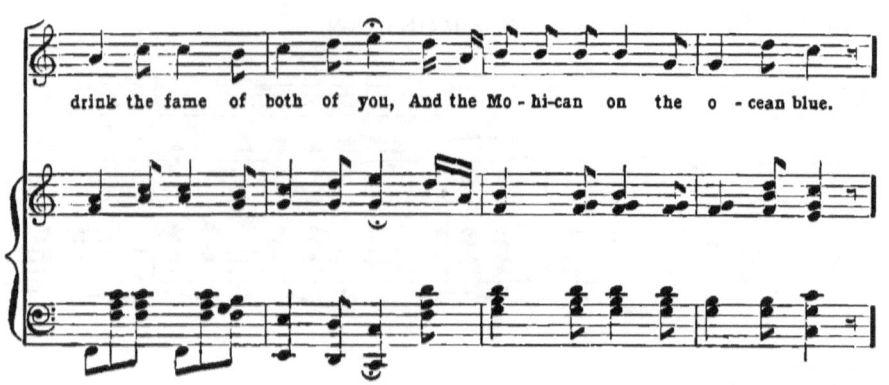

THE MOHICAN

drink to thee in ev-'ry brew, And the Mo-hi-can on the o-cean blue.

CHORUS.

Drink, drink, drink, A Mo-hi-can sails the sea, . . Drink, drink,

Drink, drink, drink, A Mo-hi-can sails the sea, . . Drink, drink,

Drink, drink, drink, A Mo-hi-can sails the sea, . . Drink, drink,

Drink, drink, drink, A Mo-hi-can sails the sea, . . Drink, drink,

AYE, AYE, SIR

SAILING OFF THE WIND

SAILING OFF THE WIND

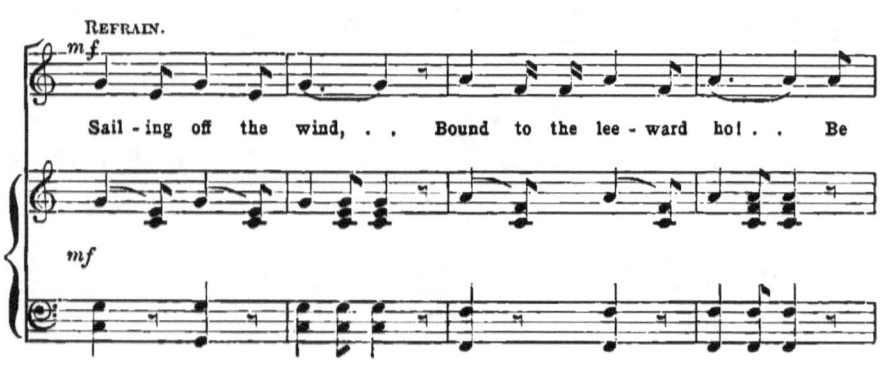

SAILING OFF THE WIND

SAILING OFF THE WIND

SAILING OFF THE WIND

He starts with joy, 'Tis land a-boy! Sail-ing off the wind...

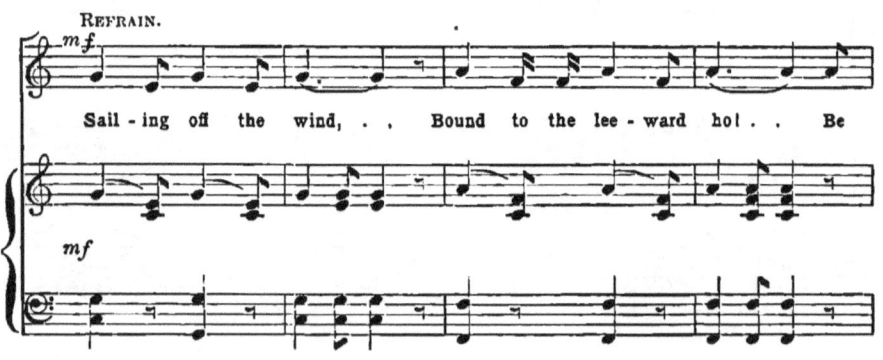

REFRAIN.
Sail-ing off the wind,.. Bound to the lee-ward ho!.. Be

mer-ry with song, As we bowl a-long, Sail-ing off the wind...

THE GIG SONG

THE GIG SONG

VIEW FROM THE ALPS

THE MASTER'S WALTZES

THE MASTER'S WALTZES

No. 1.

THE MASTER'S WALTZES

No. 2.
INTRODUCTION. WALTZ.

THE MASTER'S WALTZES

THE MASTER'S WALTZES

THE MASTER'S WALTZES

THE CHEBACCO WALTZ

THE CHEBACCO WALTZ

THE CHEBACCO WALTZ

THE CHEBACCO WALTZ

THE CHEBACCO WALTZ

THE CHEBACCO WALTZ

THE HUNTSMAN'S WALTZ

THE HUNTSMAN'S WALTZ

THE HUNTSMAN'S WALTZ

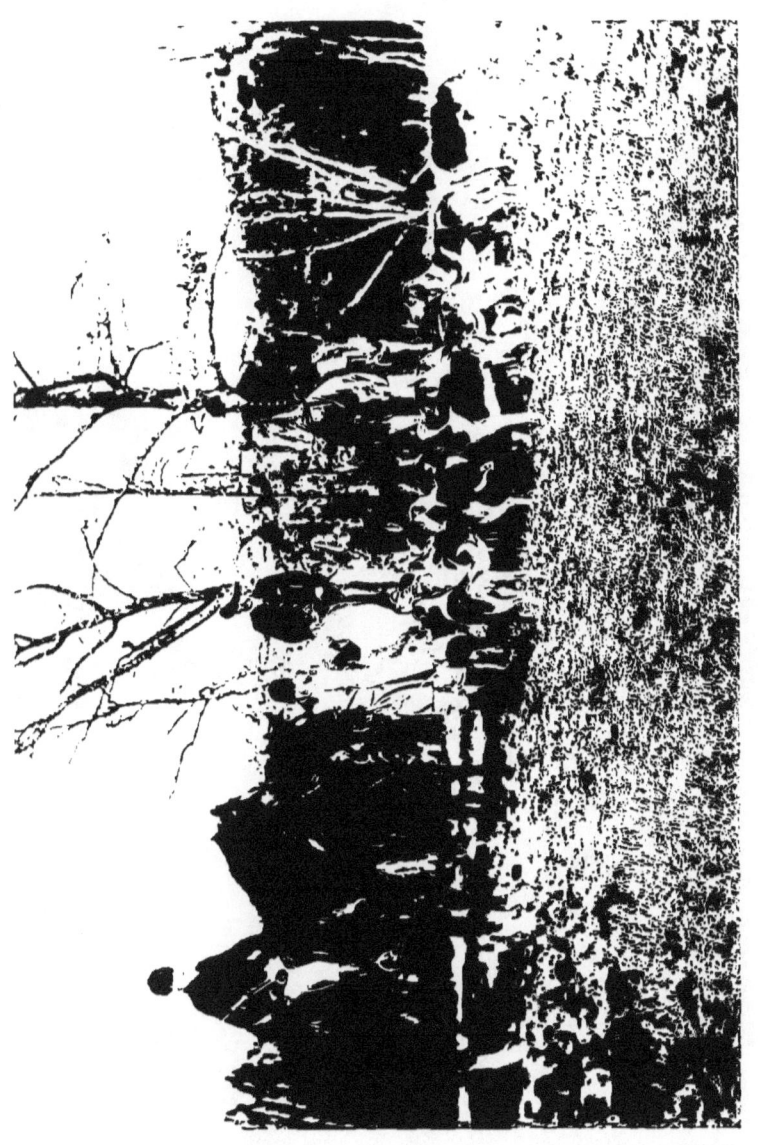

HUNT SERVANTS

KENNEL WALTZES

KENNEL WALTZES

KENNEL WALTZES

KENNEL WALTZES
No. 2.

KENNEL WALTZES

No. 3.
INTRODUCTION.

KENNEL WALTZES

KENNEL WALTZES

KENNEL WALTZES

MR. SH... AND THE AUTHOR

THE REYNARD WALTZ

THE REYNARD WALTZ

THE REYNARD WALTZ

THE REYNARD WALTZ

THE REYNARD WALTZ

THE REYNARD WALTZ

THE REYNARD WALTZ

THE REYNARD WALTZ

THE REYNARD WALTZ

MYOPIA POLKA

MYOPIA POLKA

MYOPIA POLKA

MYOPIA POLKA

www.ingramcontent.com/pod-product-compliance
Lightning Source LLC
Chambersburg PA
CBHW020806230426
43666CB00007B/877